IN THE PROMISED LAND

LIVES OF JEWISH AMERICANS

BY DOREEN RAPPAPORT
ILLUSTRATED BY CORNELIUS VAN WRIGHT
AND YING-HWA HU

HARPERCOLLINSPUBLISHERS

AUTHOR'S NOTE

More than a hundred years ago, my grandparents fled Poland and Russia for the United States. They wanted to live where they would not be punished, beaten, or even murdered because they were Jews. They wanted the freedom to practice their religion.

My grandparents were not the first Jews who fled persecution and violence. On September 1, 1654, the *Sainte Catherine* landed in the Dutch colony of New Amsterdam, now called Manhattan. On board the ship were twenty-three Jews—four men, six women, and thirteen children. Their families originally came from Spain and Portugal. During the Inquisition, in 1492, Jews were expelled from Spain; nine years later they were expelled from Portugal. Many went to live in Brazil. In 1654 the Portuguese recaptured Brazil. Jews living there fled to Holland and to the Caribbean Islands. The twenty-three people on the *Sainte Catherine* became the first permanent community of Jews in the United States.

By 1790 about two thousand Jews lived in Philadelphia, Pennsylvania; Savannah, Georgia; Charleston, South Carolina; New Haven, Connecticut; Newport, Rhode Island; and New York City. The 1830s and 1840s saw the arrival of more than two hundred thousand German Jews. From the 1880s to the 1920s, more than two million Jews from Eastern Europe fled anti-Semitic violence to make a new life in the United States.

Each wave of immigrants found themselves barred, by unwritten law or by law, from certain professions, schools, neighborhoods, and organizations. They fought to break through these barriers and carved out their own areas of achievement. Jewish women faced the double exclusion of religion and sex.

This book re-creates one moment in the lives of thirteen Jewish Americans who affected American and world history.

CONTENTS

ASSER LEVY

C. 1628-1682

Asser Levy stared at the blank paper on his desk. He knew what he had to do. He had to fight Governor Peter Stuyvesant's latest decision against the Jews in New Amsterdam. This was not the first time the governor had unfairly treated Asser's people. Nor did Asser think it would be the last time.

When Asser and twenty-two other Jews had arrived penniless from Brazil last September 1, 1654, Stuyvesant wrote to Holland for permission to kick them out. He insisted that since they had no money, the colony would have to support them. Permission was refused.

Stuyvesant had made life for the Jews as difficult as possible. He barred them from retail trade and the fur trade. They could not buy land or build homes or a place of worship. They could not vote or hold public office. Now he had refused to let them serve in the colony's militia, and insisted that they pay a special tax instead.

Asser thought the idea outrageous and unjust. He could handle a rifle as well as any man in the colony.

He wrote to the New Amsterdam council that the tax was unfair. The council turned his petition down. He wrote another petition, and another, until he was allowed to serve with the local troops.

Asser Levy became a successful businessman and respected citizen. He continued fighting unfair treatment. Little by little his petitions chipped away at anti-Semitic laws in the colony.

ERNESTINE ROSE
1810-1892

Ernestine Rose felt chilly and tired on this brutally cold February day in 1854. In the last twenty-one days, she had made twenty-one speeches in almost as many towns. In a few minutes she would speak to lawmakers in New York State. She wondered if they would boo her. Most men hated what she said.

The assembly was packed. Some women had taken seats usually reserved for the lawmakers. Others stood in the aisles and in the back of the room and spilled out into the lobby. The lawmakers sat where their clerks usually sat. Ernestine looked out at their somber faces and listed her demands: Laws had to be changed to give women the same rights as men. If divorced, women should have custody of their children. They should be entitled to vote.

The men shifted uncomfortably in their seats. The women nodded approval.

Ernestine held up petitions signed by thousands of women. "Gentlemen, these are not the demands of the moment or the few. They are the demands of the age." The chamber echoed with women's applause. The lawmakers fumed in silence.

The lawmakers did not change the laws that year. Ernestine Rose kept traveling from city to city, rallying Americans to the cause of women's rights. Gradually, child custody laws were changed. But it was not until 1920 that women won the right to vote.

SOLOMON NUNES CARVALHO
1815-1897

It was thirty degrees below zero near the Green River in what is now Utah. The snow was coming down faster and thicker now. Solomon's every step was an effort. His back ached. One foot was so badly frozen he could barely walk. Oh, how he wished he could ride, but the animals were carrying supplies for the expedition. John Frémont was mapping out a railroad route through the Rocky Mountains. He had hired Solomon to take daguerreotypes of the terrain. Solomon had already taken more than three hundred images.

Solomon fell farther and farther behind the expedition until he could no longer see the other men or the trail. Darkness settled in. The distant howling of wolves pierced the white silence. His whole body felt frozen. Now the snow was up to his knees. He sat down on a snowbank to rest. The howling was closer now. The blizzard would not keep the wolves away. He checked his gun and looked at the miniature daguerreotypes of his family. Would he ever see them again? He forced himself to get up. Finally at ten o'clock at night, he reached the camp.

Fearing his men would die, Frémont abandoned the expedition. Everything was buried in the snow so the men could ride on the animals. No one ever returned to get anything.

When Solomon returned home, he invented three apparatuses to make steam boilers more efficient. He became wealthy.

JACOB W. DAVIS
1834-1908

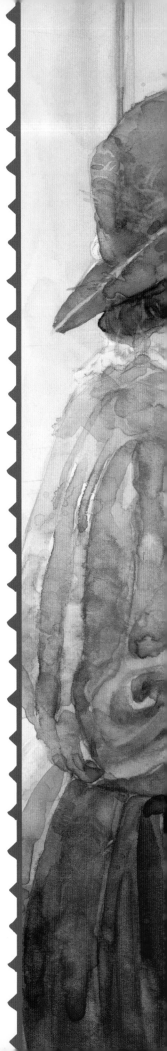

Jacob looked up at the woman in his tailor shop on Virginia Street in Reno, Nevada. Her husband was mining for gold. He needed new waist overalls, but he was too big for ready-made clothing. She held out two strings with knots. The knots marked her husband's waist size and the width of his upper thighs. Jacob agreed to make him overalls for three dollars.

He cut out a pants pattern on stiff canvas. Then he stitched the pants together with orange thread. Now, to stitch the pockets onto the pants. Miners' pockets had to be strong enough to hold small nuggets and gold dust. Thread wasn't sturdy enough. What could he use? Maybe copper rivets.

He pushed tiny rivets through the pocket corners and fastened them on the other side. He pulled on the pockets. The copper rivets worked. The pockets did not come apart now.

The miners loved Jacob's waist overalls with the rivets. He worried that someone might steal his idea. On July 2, 1872, he wrote to Levi Strauss, who sold him material. He offered to go into partnership with Levi if he would pay the $68 patent fee. Levi agreed.

Business exploded as cowboys and lumberjacks discovered these long-lasting pants. Jacob supervised manufacturing in the Levi Strauss factory until he died. Today people all over the world wear Levi Strauss jeans, originally created by Jacob W. Davis.

LILLIAN WALD
1867-1940

Lillian was a nurse, studying to be a doctor. As part of her training, she taught nursing skills to immigrant mothers. Today's lesson was in making a bed. She tucked the sheet tightly under the mattress and felt a tug at her skirt. "My mother is sick." A little girl babbled on. Lillian realized that her mother had just given birth. Class would have to wait. She gathered medical supplies and rushed out into the drizzly March air.

The girl led Lillian through muddy streets in New York City's Lower East Side. Hanging upside down from stalls were chickens and slabs of rotten meat. Children were playing on dirty mattresses and around uncovered garbage cans. Lillian heard bits of Yiddish as she wended her way through people and food and refuse. She had not known that Jews lived in such slums.

The girl led her into a brick tenement, up stairs slimy with mud and garbage, and into a room crammed with six children and two adults. The mother lay on a filthy board. No one should live this way, Lillian thought. She sent the girl to boil water. Then she took her patient in her arms to clean her and her newborn baby.

Lillian did not return to medical school that March of 1893. She rented a building on Henry Street. She hired nurses to care for people in their homes. By 1915 her Visiting Nurse Service was making 227,000 visits a year. The Henry Street Settlement still helps people build better lives for themselves.

HARRY HOUDINI (EHRICH WEISS)

1874-1926

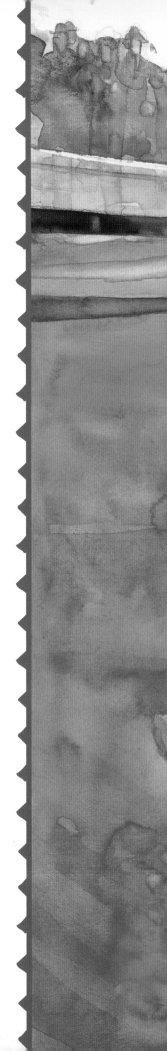

Ten thousand people were jammed together near the Mississippi River for a free performance of the Manacled Bridge Jump by the great Houdini. The spectators in New Orleans, Louisiana, watched the thirty-three-year-old magician slowly take off his coat and vest and unclip his suspenders. He unbuttoned his dress shirt. Then, out of his pants and off with his stockings. He smiled and turned his muscular body toward the cameras.

An assistant handcuffed Houdini behind his back. Irons chained to the handcuffs pulled his elbows closer together. The assistant draped another chain around his throat and chest and brought it toward his back. Houdini's wrists were then bound together. The ends of the chain were locked around his throat.

"Good-bye, boys," his voice boomed. He jumped feet first into the cold, dark water. Five seconds. Ten seconds. Fifteen seconds. *How far down was he?* Twenty seconds. Twenty-five seconds. *Was he still breathing?* Thirty seconds. *Would he escape from his manacles in time?*

Suddenly an arm holding chains and locks stuck up from the water. Then Houdini's head appeared, and thousands cheered.

Houdini's magic dazzled the world. He escaped from handcuffs, chains, jail cells, and packing crates. He walked through brick walls. He even made a five-ton elephant disappear. People are still trying to figure out the secrets of this great magician.

PAULINE NEWMAN
1890–1986

Pauline's fingers trembled as she trimmed threads from a shirt. It was too cold to work a second longer by the broken window. She ran across the splintered floor of the Triangle Shirtwaist Factory, past rows of women stooped over sewing machines. Reaching the stove, she stuck out her fingers to warm them.

"Get back to work," the foreman yelled. Pauline rushed back to the corner where she worked fifteen hours a day. She hated her low-paying job, but her family would starve without it.

"Quick, into the boxes," someone shouted. Pauline knew an inspector was in the factory looking for children. It was ten o'clock at night. It was against the law for children to be working. She scrambled into a big box. Another girl jumped in beside her. Someone piled shirts over them. More shirts were piled on top of the box. Pauline held her breath.

Pauline decided that the only way to change working conditions was for workers to band together in a union. In 1909, when she was nineteen, she helped lead a strike of twenty thousand garment workers in New York City. The women protested their poor pay, long hours, and unsafe working conditions. They won the strike, but they did not get everything they asked for.

For seventy years Pauline Newman worked for the ILGWU, the International Ladies Garment Workers' Union, as an organizer, journalist, and educator.

LILLIAN COPELAND
1904-1964

Last chance to win an Olympic gold medal. At the Games four years ago, in 1928, Lillian Copeland had won a silver medal. She wanted gold this time.

She readied for her last throw. She encircled the rim with the last joints on her fingers. Her thumb was flat. Her grip felt right. She bent her legs and shifted her weight to her rear foot. Her stance felt right. Most discus throwers pivot and turn to gain momentum for their throw. Lillian threw straight. Back, forward. Back, forward. She swung her right arm. Her arm muscles felt loose and ready. *Now, let go!* The throw felt right. She watched the heavy metal discus fly through the air.

"Lillian Copeland, 133 feet and 1 5/8 inches," the announcer's voice boomed over the microphones. Tears streamed down her face. She had captured the gold, setting a new world record.

From 1925 to 1932 Lillian Copeland won nine national championships, setting six world records in the shot put, javelin, and discus throw. She won in all three categories at the Second World Maccabiah Games in Palestine in 1935. She planned to try for a second gold medal at the 1936 Olympics. But she did not compete. It was her protest against Nazi dictator Adolf Hitler, who refused to let German Jews play on their team.

In 1994 Lillian Copeland was elected into the United States Track and Field Hall of Fame.

IRA HIRSCHMANN
1901-1989

Ira Hirschmann's eyes were fixed on the 758 people jammed onto a ship meant to hold 300 people. The children numbered 256. The passengers on the *Kazbek* were Romanian Jews who had escaped from concentration camps in their country. Under dictator Adolf Hitler, millions of Jews had already been murdered or starved to death in such camps.

Ira saw children's bony hands clinging to the ropes on the side of the ship. Their long, sallow faces with tired, frightened eyes peered out at him, begging for help. This was not the first time Jews had fled to Turkey so they would not be killed. Turkish officials usually refused to let these "illegal" refugees enter their country, where they could continue by train to Palestine. Each time Ira had argued and pleaded for help for the refugees. He did not always succeed. But today, July 9, 1944, he had triumphed.

His rowboat was now only a few feet from the *Kazbek*. He wanted to race onto the ship and hug the children. Turkish officials had forbidden him to board the *Kazbek*. But they couldn't stop him from shouting the good news. "You're safe now," he yelled over and over again. "You're safe now."

During World War II, Ira Hirschmann left his comfortable life as an executive to work for the War Refugee Board. He saved nearly seven thousand Hungarian, Romanian, and Bulgarian Jews.

JONAS SALK
1914-1995

"How are you? What have you been up to?" Dr. Jonas Salk greeted the children in the D. T. Watson Home for Crippled Children in Leetsdale, Pennsylvania. These children were helping him in his first tests to create a polio vaccine.

Every year polio infected tens of thousands of people all over the world. Most became temporarily weak and then recovered. Some became permanently paralyzed. These forty-three children had recovered from polio. Their parents had agreed to let Jonas test his vaccine on them even though it was risky.

Slowly he drew the liquid vaccine into a hypodermic needle. He spoke softly to sixteen-year-old William Kirkpatrick. He didn't want William to be afraid. He explained that he would inject a small amount of the polio virus into William's body. Salk hoped that would produce antibodies to fight and kill the virus. He dabbed alcohol on William's arm and gently stuck the needle in. William did not flinch.

Jonas hardly slept in the next thirty days of that summer of 1952 as he waited for the test results. The vaccine worked.

Next he tried out the vaccine on people who had not had polio, including himself, his wife, and children. Then there were mass trials on one million children. It worked. By 1959 ninety-one countries used Salk's vaccine. His research led another scientist, Albert Sabin, to produce an even more effective polio vaccine.

RUTH BADER GINSBURG
1933-

Ruth looked at the list of law journals in the library. The one she needed wasn't here. It was probably at Lamont Library. She hurried across the Harvard campus.

"You can't come in here," a guard said. "Women are not allowed." There were only nine women among the five hundred law students in her class. They often heard the words *you can't.* Since Ruth was little, people had told her, "You can't, because you're a girl." Luckily her mother had told her *she could.* But she still felt angry when she heard these words.

"Well, I'll stand at the door and you can bring me the journal," she said to the guard. He refused. She had no choice but to leave.

When Ruth graduated from law school in 1959, she was tied for first place in her class. Not one law firm offered her a job. She was not surprised. Most law firms did not hire Jews or women. She was recommended to clerk for Supreme Court Justice Felix Frankfurter. He refused to even meet her.

Ruth decided the *you can'ts* had to stop. She went to court to challenge laws that discriminated against women. She argued five cases before the U.S. Supreme Court. She won all five. People began to take notice of her fine legal mind.

In 1980 Ruth Ginsburg was appointed to the U.S. Court of Appeals for the District of Columbia. In 1993 she became the second woman justice to serve on the U.S. Supreme Court.

JUDITH RESNICK
1949-1986

One of the astronauts laughed and pointed to Judith's hair. Up in space with zero gravity, her dark brown curls rose like corkscrews. Judith grinned as he took her photograph. Then she returned to work. Her job on her first shuttle mission was to unfold a solar-powered sail in space.

She turned the *Discovery*'s gigantic remote-control arm. Judith had practiced manipulating this arm so many times it felt like part of her body. She watched the sail's panels of super-thin plastic come out of the cargo bay. The panels were pleated like an accordion. They unfolded slowly until all eighty-four were open. The 120-foot solar sail sat like a giant fan atop the spaceship. It was the largest structure ever set up in space.

"It's up and it's big," she reported to Mission Control. "It's very steady and stable. No wobbling."

She saw sunlight strike the sail, making it glisten like gold. The sail converted sunlight to electricity. Future solar sails might make enough electricity to run a permanent space station.

Engineer Judith Resnick was chosen from among eight thousand people to become the second American woman in space. On the 1984 *Discovery* mission, she logged 144 hours and 57 minutes in space. She died two years later on the tragic *Challenger* mission, which claimed the lives of six astronauts and one teacher.

STEVEN SPIELBERG
1946-

Steven sat at a drawing board, creating the star of his next movie, *E.T.: The Extra-Terrestrial.* What should E.T. look like? E.T. was a lovable alien accidentally left behind on Earth by his kin. How should he feel? Lonely, Steven thought. Steven knew about loneliness. As a boy he was lonely much of the time. At school kids had hit and taunted him because he was Jewish.

E.T. must be lovable and innocent-looking, and yet be old, he decided. He pasted the eyes of poet Carl Sandburg onto a baby's face. He glued on the wrinkled forehead of the writer Ernest Hemingway. Down went the nose of the scientist Albert Einstein. Now for E.T.'s neck. It would stretch so he could look around corners. If E.T. got scared, his neck could shrink and help him hide like a turtle under its shell. In movie theaters all over the world, people rooted for E.T. to find his way home.

Steven Spielberg has produced more than fifty movies and directed twenty-one feature films. He has won two Oscars for best director for *Saving Private Ryan* and *Schindler's List.* He considers *Schindler's List* his most important film. It tells the story of German Oskar Schindler, who rescued more than twelve hundred Jews during the Holocaust.

Spielberg has set up the Survivors of the Shoah Visual History Foundation. The life stories of fifty thousand survivors are now on videotape for people all over the world to see.

ABOUT THIS BOOK

WHEN I DECIDED TO WRITE A BOOK about Jewish Americans, I found many exciting, accomplished people to include.

To write defining moments in their lives, I read as many different sources as I could. I checked the sources against one another to write as true an account as possible: I read newspaper and magazine articles, interviews, diaries, journals, and books by historians who spent years researching the past. I was lucky and found first-person accounts by Pauline Newman, Ernestine Rose, Lillian Wald, Solomon Nunes Carvalho, Ira Hirschmann, Jonas Salk, Steven Spielberg, and Ruth Bader Ginsburg, describing what happened to them and how they felt. Newspaper and magazine articles described in great detail Lillian Copeland's discus throw, Judith Resnick's work on the 1984 *Discovery* mission, and Houdini's daring feat. The Jacob W. Davis website included family information and the letter that Davis wrote to Levi Strauss about his new "waist overalls." The reference librarians in the Jewish Division of the New York Public Research Library led me to books by pioneer scholars in the history of Jewish Americans, which detailed Asser Levy's petitions.

The title *In the Promised Land* was inspired by *The Promised Land*, a memoir by Mary Antin, whose family immigrated to the United States in 1894 from Polotzk, a town in Russia.

—*Doreen Rappaport*

ILLUSTRATING LIVING AND HISTORICAL FIGURES is always a daunting challenge. How do you capture the essence of a person in one illustration? How do you do justice to what the person has accomplished? It was not easy to find images of all the people featured in this book. Sometimes we uncovered few visual clues to what they looked like. For this reason and sometimes for the sake of creating our art, we took license with several of the portrayals. For instance, researching how Asser Levy would have looked was difficult. Photography did not exist in the seventeenth century, and we found no portraits of him, so we relied on etchings of people and the attire of that period to guess what he may have looked like. In the end we hope that we have helped illuminate the accomplishments of these thirteen great Americans.

—*Cornelius Van Wright and Ying-Hwa Hu*

SELECTED RESEARCH SOURCES

Antin, Mary. *The Promised Land.* Boston: Houghton Mifflin, 1912.

Babcock, Muriel. "Lillian Copeland Closes Athletic Career in Glory." *Los Angeles Times*, August 3, 1932.

Baxter, John. *Steven Spielberg.* New York: HarperCollins, 1996.

Campbell, Anne Morgan. "In Nineteenth Century Nevada: Federal Records as Sources for Local History." *Nevada Historical Society Quarterly*, Fall 1974.

Carter, Richard. *Breakthrough: The Saga of Jonas Salk.* New York: Trident Press, 1965.

Carvalho, Solomon Nunes. *Travels and Incidents in the Far West with Col. Fremont's Last Expedition.* New York: Derby & Jackson, 1857.

Hershkowitz, Leo. "Original Inventions of Early New York Jews (1682–1763)." *American Jewish History*, Volume 90, Number 3, September 2002.

Hirschmann, Ira. *Caution to the Winds.* New York: David McKay, 1962.

Marcus, Jacob Rader. *The Colonial American Jew, 1492–1776.* Detroit: Wayne State University Press, 1970.

Oreleck, Annelise. *Common Sense and a Little Fire: Women and Working-class Politics in the United States, 1900–1965.* Chapel Hill: University of North Carolina Press, 1995.

Schoener, Allan. *American Jewish Album.* New York: Rizzoli, 1983.

Silverman, Kenneth. *Houdini! The Career of Ehrich Weiss: Self-liberator, Europe's Eclipsing Sensation, World's Handcuff King & Prison Breaker.* New York: HarperCollins, c1996.

Suhl, Yuri. *Ernestine Rose and the Battle for Human Rights.* New York: Reynal, 1959.

Wald, Lillian. *The House on Henry Street.* New York: Henry Holt, 1915.

www.bendavis.com/home/davis.html

www.levistrauss.com/about/history/jeans.htm

BOOKS AND WEBSITES FOR YOUNG READERS

Baxter, John. *Steven Spielberg.* New York: HarperCollins, 1996.

Hargrove, Jim. *The Story of Jonas Salk and the Discovery of the Polio Vaccine.* New York: Scholastic Library Publishing, 1990.

Hirschberger, Arlene B. *Photo Odyssey: Solomon Carvalho's Remarkable Western Adventure 1853–54.* New York: Clarion Books, 2000.

Jones, Brenn. *Learning about Equal Rights from the Life of Ruth Bader Ginsburg.* New York: Rosen Publishing Group, 2002.

Lalicki, Tom. *Spellbinder: The Life of Harry Houdini.* New York: Holiday House, 2000.

Littlefield, Holly. *Fire at the Triangle Factory.* Illustrated by Mary O'Keefe Young. Minneapolis: Carolrhoda, 1996.

Roberts, Jack L. *Ruth Bader Ginsburg: Supreme Court Justice.* Brookfield, Ct.: Millbrook Press, 1994.

Weidt, Maryann N. *Mr. Blue Jeans: A Story About Levi Strauss.* Illustrated by Lydia M. Anderson. Minneapolis: Carolrhoda Books, First Avenue Editions, 1992.

www.ajhs.org/about/sport.cfm (Jews in sports)

www.us-israel.org/jsource/biography/rose.html (Ernestine Rose)

www.amuseum.org/jahf (Jewish American Hall of Fame)

www.pbs.org/weta/thewest/people/s_z/strauss.htm (Levi Strauss)

www.time.com/time/time100/scientist/profile/salk.html (Jonas Salk)

For Ryan Rosegarten, the biographer of Murray T. Finsdale —D.R.

To our dear friends Masahiro and Kaori —C.V.W. and Y.-H.H.

Jewish poet Emma Lazarus (1849–1887) wrote "The New Colossus." The sonnet is engraved on the pedestal of the Statue of Liberty. "'Give me your tired, your poor,/ Your huddled masses yearning to breathe free'" still inspires immigrants who come to the United States.

In the Promised Land • Text copyright © 2005 by Doreen Rappaport • Illustrations copyright © 2005 by Cornelius Van Wright and Ying-Hwa Hu • Manufactured in China by Toppan Printing Company Ltd. • All rights reserved. • www.harperchildrens.com Library of Congress Cataloging-in-Publication Data • Rappaport, Doreen. • In the promised land : lives of Jewish Americans / by Doreen Rappaport ; illustrated by Cornelius Van Wright and Ying-Hwa Hu.—1st ed. • p. cm • Summary: Offers vignettes from the lives of thirteen Jewish Americans whose achievements, from the colonial period through the present, contributed to women's and worker's rights, medicine, science, fashion, photography, sport, and entertainment. • ISBN 0-688-17150-8—ISBN 0-06-059395-4 (lib. bdg.) • 1. Jews—United States—Biography—Juvenile literature. [1. Jews—United States—Biography.] I. Van Wright, Cornelius, ill. II. Hu, Ying-Hwa, ill. III. Title. E184.37.A168 2005 • 920'.0092924073—dc22 • 2003023011 • Designed by Stephanie Bart-Horvath • 1 2 3 4 5 6 7 8 9 10

❖

First Edition